Why Animals Live in Caves

By Valerie J. Weber

Reading consultant:

Susan Nations, M.Ed., *author/literacy coach/consultant in literacy development*

Science and curriculum consultant:

Debra Voege, M.A., *science curriculum resource teacher*

WEEKLY READER®
PUBLISHING

Please visit our web site at www.garethstevens.com.
For a free color catalog describing our list of high-quality books, call 1-800-542-2595 (USA) or 1-800-387-3178 (Canada). Our fax: 1-877-542-2596

Library of Congress Cataloging-in-Publication Data
Weber, Valerie.
    Why animals live in caves / by Valerie J. Weber.
      p. cm. — (Where animals live)
    Includes bibliographical references and index.
    ISBN-10: 0-8368-8794-8   ISBN-13: 978-0-8368-8794-5 (lib. bdg. : alk. paper)
    ISBN-10: 0-8368-8801-4   ISBN-13: 978-0-8368-8801-0 (softcover)
    1. Cave animals—Juvenile literature. 2. Caves—Juvenile literature.
  3. Animals—Habitations—Juvenile literature.
  I. Title.
  QL117.W44   2008
  591.75'84—dc22   2007042514

This edition first published in 2008 by
Weekly Reader® Books
An Imprint of Gareth Stevens Publishing
1 Reader's Digest Road
Pleasantville, NY 10570-7000 USA

Copyright © 2008 by Gareth Stevens, Inc.

Senior Managing Editor: Lisa M. Guidone
Senior Editor: Barbara Bakowski
Creative Director: Lisa Donovan
Senior Designer: Keith Plechaty
Production Designer: Amy Ray, *Studio Montage*
Photo Researcher: Diane Laska-Swanke

Photo Credits: Cover © Ken Lucas/Visuals Unlimited; pp. 1, 3, 6 © Photodisc; p. 5 © Hermann Brehm/ naturepl.com; p. 7 Diane Blasius; p. 8 © Adam Jones/Visuals Unlimited; p. 9 © Joseph T. Collins/Photo Researchers, Inc.; p. 11 © Gerry Ellis/Minden Pictures; p. 12 © Christian Ziegler/Minden Pictures; p. 13 © Dr. Merlin D. Tuttle/Bat Conservation International/Photo Researchers, Inc.; p. 14 © Jose B. Ruiz/naturepl.com; p. 15 © Dietmar Nill/Foto Natura/Minden Pictures; pp. 17, 18 © Fred Bavendam/Minden Pictures; p. 19 © WaterFrame/Alamy; p. 20 © Brandon Cole/Visuals Unlimited; p. 21 © Wolfgang Kaehler

Printed in the United States of America

1 2 3 4 5 6 7 8 9 10 09 08 07

Table of Contents

Words that appear in the glossary are printed in **boldface** type the first time they occur in the text.

Chapter 1

Safety in Caves

You may think of caves as dark and gloomy places. You would be right. You may think that no person or animal could live in a cave. You would be wrong about that.

Caves can be a good place to raise a family. In some countries, many people live in caves.

A lot of animals spend all or part of their lives in caves. Caves shelter them in bad weather and protect them from **predators**. Predators are animals that hunt and eat other animals.

Female cougars (KOO-gerz) sometimes give birth and raise their young in caves.

Chapter 2

Kinds of Caves

A cave is an opening into the ground. Caves can be huge, with long **passages** between big rooms. Caves can also be small cracks in rocks. There are caves on land and caves in the ocean.

Caves on land are divided into three zones. The entrance zone is the part of the cave that opens to the surface. Animals that come and go in the cave often live in this zone. Beetles, snakes, earthworms, and small rodents live in the entrance zone.

Most caves are lined with rock.

entrance zone

twilight zone

dark zone

The **twilight** zone is just beyond the entrance zone. Twilight is the time just after sunset or just before sunrise when the light in the sky is dim. Little light enters this zone, which is cool and damp. Cave crickets and cave beetles live in the twilight zone.

Cave crickets often leave the cave to find food.

The dark zone lies deep in the cave. No light reaches this area. Only animals that can live in the dark stay here. Some of them have no eyes, since there is no light to see with.

Many animals that live in the dark zone are colorless, like this Texas blind salamander.

Chapter 3

Bat Caves

Bats spend much of the day sleeping in dark, sheltered places. Some bats live in barns or attics. Others live in trees or even hide under leaves.

Many large groups of bats live in caves. Several thousand bats may live in the same cave. They hang upside down by their feet. Their claws cling to the rough roof of the cave.

Hanging upside down in a cave, this bat is safe from its predators.

Gray bats sleep in the cave during the day. They may clean their fur and wings or take care of their young. Bats hunt for food at night.

In winter, some bats **hibernate**. They enter a deep sleep and are inactive both during the day and at night. They huddle together to keep warm. More than seventy-five gray bats can hang in an area the size of this book!

Large groups of fruit bats hang together in caves.

For part of the summer, mother bats may live in a separate part of the cave. They give birth to baby bats there.

Bats are **mammals**. They feed their babies with milk from their bodies.

This newborn gray bat is not ready to leave the cave.

The **temperature** of the cave affects the size of the baby bats. They grow larger in warm caves than in cool caves. When the baby bats are about two months old, they are ready to fly on their own.

This greater mouse-eared bat flies from its cave to look for food.

Bats choose caves that are close to a food source. Many bats eat insects that live near water. The bats find caves that are near streams and lakes.

A bat flies at night, snatching bugs from the air.

Chapter 4

Sea and Land Caves

Other animals live in caves in the ocean. Some fish, crabs, and **sea urchins** find holes in rocks or **coral reefs**. Even some sharks live in caves along the seafloor.

Some sea animals live in a small hole or cave for their entire life. Others leave the cave to look for food. They may hide their eggs in a cave to protect them from predators.

Pacific giant octopuses use caves to shelter their eggs. The mother octopus lays her eggs in strands, hanging them from the cave's ceiling. She then gathers rocks and shells and places them at the cave's entrance. The wall of rocks keeps predators from getting to the eggs.

A mother octopus protects her eggs.

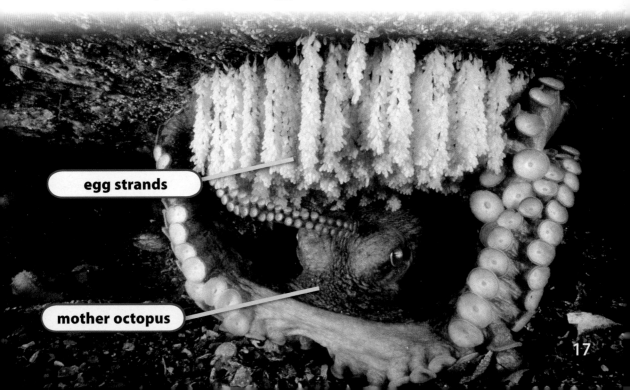

egg strands

mother octopus

The mother octopus stays in the cave with her eggs, keeping them safe. She blows water at them to keep them clean. After six months, the eggs **hatch**, releasing tiny octopuses. The mother blows them out of the cave, into open water.

Each octopus egg is the size of a grain of rice.

Banded coral shrimp also live in caves. These shrimp are "cleaners." The shrimp wait at the opening to the cave and wave their **antennae**. That movement and the shrimp's red and white bands attract fish that want to be cleaned. The shrimp gets a meal from what it picks off the fish.

The fish will not eat the shrimp, even if the shrimp enters the fish's mouth.

banded coral shrimp

Moray eels back their long, slim bodies into narrow undersea caves. They hide in the caves during the day, waiting for other fish to pass by. Then the eels dart out and grab their **prey**. At night, the moray eels leave their caves to hunt fish in the open seas.

A moray eel has sharp teeth for biting prey.

In China, millions of people live in land caves. They do so for the same reasons that animals do. The caves are warm in winter and cool in summer. They protect people from the weather. Parents can raise their children safely in caves.

You see, a cave can be a great home!

In parts of China, people dig caves in the soft dirt.

Glossary

antennae: two long feelers on the heads of insects or crustaceans (kruss-TAY-shuns), which are water animals with a hard shell

coral reefs: ridges or mounds made of coral, which is formed from the skeletons of tiny sea animals called coral polyps (PAH-lips)

hatch: to come out of an egg

hibernate: to pass the winter in a deep sleep

mammals: animals that are warm-blooded, have a backbone, and feed their babies milk made in their bodies

passages: roads, paths, or routes along which people or animals travel

predators: animals that hunt and eat other animals

prey: an animal that is hunted and eaten by other animals

sea urchins: ball-shaped ocean animals with spines

temperature: a measurement of heat or coldness

twilight: the time just after sunset or just before sunrise when the light is soft and hazy

To Find Out More

Books

Cave. Diane Siebert (HarperCollins)

Cave Animals. Animals in Their Habitats (series). Francine Galko (Heinemann)

Cave Life. Look Closer (series). DK Publishing (DK Children)

Caves. Earthforms (series). Ellen Sturm Niz (Capstone Press)

Caves: Hidden World. First Discovery Books (series). Claude Delafosse and Gallimard Jeunesse (Scholastic)

Life in a Cave. Microhabitats (series). Clare Oliver (Raintree)

Web Sites

Kidport Reference Library: Animal Homes
www.kidport.com/RefLib/Science/AnimalHomes/CaveHomes.htm
Learn about animals that live in caves.

Enchanted Learning: Caves
www.enchantedlearning.com/biomes/cave/terrestrial.shtml
See how caves are divided into zones, and find out more about the animals that call caves home.

Publisher's note to educators and parents: Our editors have carefully reviewed these web sites to ensure that they are suitable for children. Many web sites change frequently, however, and we cannot guarantee that a site's future contents will continue to meet our high standards of quality and educational value. Be advised that children should be closely supervised whenever they access the Internet.

Index

About the Author

A writer and editor for more than twenty-five years, Valerie Weber especially loves working in children's publishing. Her book topics have been endlessly engaging—from the weird wonders of the sea, to the lives of girls during World War II, to the making of movies. She is grateful to her family, including her husband and daughters, and her friends for offering their support and for listening to the odd facts she has discovered during her work. Did you know, for example, that frogs use their eyeballs to push food down into their stomachs?